Equality

A Poetic Journey

by

James Parton

1663 LIBERTY DRIVE, SUITE 200
BLOOMINGTON, INDIANA 47403
(800) 839-8640
WWW.AUTHORHOUSE.COM

© 2005 James Parton
All Rights Reserved.

No part of this book may be reproduced, stored in a retrieval system, or transmitted by any means without the written permission of the author.

First published by AuthorHouse 03/01/05

ISBN: 1-4208-0289-5 (sc)

Printed in the United States of America
Bloomington, Indiana

This book is printed on acid-free paper.

For Dad,
Who lost it all for me,
And Mom,
Who never gave up,

You gave me independence.

For Candice,
Who taught me to always be true,
And Lisa,
Who restored my pride,

You showed me the way.

For all the friends,
Who kept things the same,
And Lewis,
Who changed everything,

You made this place home.

~ *Prologue* ~

Equality; it is something that we inevitably strive for as human beings.

We search for equality in our journeys, finding times to venture out and times to stay put; between mankind, to find a common ground for happiness to flourish; and in love, finding an identity in another that molds with our own.

We achieve equality in our experience of pain, as it insists upon matching our pleasure; in our very beings, as mind. body, and soul create something greater than we've ever known to understand; and the world, as a place where these feelings live indefinitely, and hold us to the promises we may never have made, but truly wish to fulfill.

Such is the role of this single word, with more than a million purposes, equally difficult to obtain. Sometimes equality will come to us naturally; occasionally we'll have to fight for it. Simple as it may seem, it can take a lifetime to figure out just what to do at the right time.

This journey opens up to pleasure and pain, the dark and light, and those things beautiful and grotesque; a tour de force of our minds, that touch so many places in time to get a taste of equality, and continue to search even now.

> *You hold in your hands an account*
> *Of life's different joys and pains;*
> *A chronicle of equality*
> *In our minds, bodies, souls,*
> *And most certainly our struggling world*

Equality

He was standing there,
In the midst of a twilight moon,
Atop the grandest hill.

My mind was fearful,
My body shook anxiously,
But my soul reached out to this man.
It said to me, "Go forth."
"Encounter what you aspire to be."

I calmed my mind,
I steadied my body,
And my soul smiled;
For controlling myself was important,
If I was to be like this man,
Of unyielding courage and determined will.

I crept forward,
Still cautious of my mind's instincts,
And joined him atop this place
That he alone had made sacred.

We spoke for hours, without saying a word,
Watching the sun set upon the horizon.
Eventually, he turned to walk away,
But stopped.

"It was nice meeting you," he said,
Before resuming his trek.
I said nothing back.
I couldn't.

Not because of my body, or my mind,
But because it filled me with glee,
Down within my soul,
That this powerful man, who yielded to no one,
Saw me as an equal,
For I now understood, what he knew so well.

I stood atop the grandest hill,
In the midst of a twilight moon,
And from behind me came another,
Who was strong of will.

Equality

~ *Journeys* ~

"The gem cannot be polished without friction, nor man perfected without trials."

– *Chinese proverb*

James Parton

Equality

Smile upon Your Fate

The wind blows softly,
Making the trees above dance,
For today, as responses echo in the air,
An epic truth unfolds upon the unsuspecting.

In many ways,
Life is a semblance of death;
We choose those who accompany us,
Yet ultimately end up alone.

Some find this to be sad, torn with irony,
But death smiles upon us all,
And all that the strong among us can do,
Is smile back.

James Parton

Your Coming Day

Mind apart, but not astray,
Searching for information anew,
Whence the appendages of desire,
Reach far and wide.

Yet may be your coming day,
Evolution striking the change,
Yet sealing your death;

For better or worse, all days will live,
Solely to die once again.

Equality

Blackened Sun

Cursed to live eternal pain,
To look upon these shadows, vain,

Whenever shrieks were heard above,
So you took to a blackened sun.

It's dark façade, who's dimly lit,
Shines on all, in spite of it,

With newborn light from summer's past,
That lives to lie upon the last;

The last of those who watch the world,
The last that lie amassed.

James Parton

Surrounded

Darkened wood, so there you stood,
And wept your days away,
Your eyes spoke silently of the truth,
You thought not once to stray.

If moonlight bide be only light,
The warming glow may sunlight fight,
In jealousy or envy green;
Neither fails to set the scene.

To turn your mind to set and rest,
The creatures here propose their test,
Among the darkness, past the leaves,
Their blood red eyes show enmity.

In desperation for your soul,
Your spirit merely be their toll,
Could pay to get you through the night,
Forever steal away your light.

Equality

<u>Air</u>

It stood that he was young,
Unabated in unawareness,
Facing a future forcing out.

It would come in summer,
He would come at night,
To settle so dispensed and lost,

A pest mettle in name,
To a child, still a game,
Cost meddlesome and roundabout,

To make it out, not raising shouts and,
Unsupported, alone he goes,
Sound and disturbances left at rest,

.

.Coming still at night, as best,
She came with haste, reluctant too,
Danger surrounding, clouded,

Shrouded in its continue,
Of an equally clouted venue,
Encompassing only two.

Thus begins an gripping tale,
That could all lead to naught,
With just misjudged thought.

James Parton

The Tower

The tower stood there,
Impervious, impassible.

The dark night sky only contributed,
To the fear one would feel,
When glancing upon its majesty.

The gargoyles perched upon every sill,
Demons, turned to stone,
By the deterioration of time.

Who dared to enter?
To challenge it's might?
I did, I did!

Nothing scared me; I considered it a strength.
Or maybe a weakness, since I was too brave,
Or too stupid to know when to stop.

I stared into the gargoyle's lifeless eyes,
Hearing their screams of pain,
And opened the doors to face my destiny.

It was dark inside, not a surprise.
But sight or naught, I had to continue.
Someone waited for me, and I couldn't let him down.

Equality

The tower stood there, impervious, impassible;
    But I had entered,
   And I would exit just as well.

James Parton

Equality

~ *Between Man* ~

"Dreams can be difficult to pursue, but the people we pursue them with can make the unattainable experiences possible."

– James Parton

James Parton

Equality

Take No Heed

Of charge to spin
To through and through,
All we choose,
And process do.

We do what we want,
To often need,
But to which point,
Need we take heed?

Within my ears,
Disappointed shouts.
To leave sins in dear,
Or get on out.

I have no heed to take with you,
Nor challenge here, no bout.

James Parton

<u>Request</u>

Wouldn't I do,
Wouldn't I not,
Making decisions,
Cannot be taught.

You await my answer,
While distressed,
The only one,
Who can grant your request.

Equality

Dates!

Date, a date!
Those things I hate, yet fancy in mind so fond.

They're fun and all, I will admit,
The company so grand,
But oftentimes, the nervousness,
Is quite hard to disband.

The jitters, my nerves,
Butterflies from below,
My stomach feels sick,
But still I know,

You'll be just as nervous as me my dear,
Your cheeks a radiant glow.

James Parton

<u>Fight</u>

In the dead of night,
I saw the fight,
Witnessed exchanging fools,

One hit the floor,
Two half made blows,
Three sickly indented wounds;

Between the two,
Indecisive to whom,
Received to each untrue.

Triumph

My knuckles scarred,
The skin near gone,
While arms in harmony,
Blaze with energy.

My lungs contract,
Breath choked from my build,
While legs go numb,
And crumple beneath me.

Yet,
As I lose consciousness,
I cry out inside:
"I've triumphed."

James Parton

Rules of Battle

Sins among the heavens sealed,
Give basis for all we hold dear,
On paths untouched with bravery,

Conviction remains apart from fear.

Along the barricaded walls,
Where these battered gates speak simply,
Victory requires sacrifice.

Impossibilities rule with harmony.

Frantic running transparent foes,
Facing in line and dramatic,
A feeling can creep upon the mind.

The truest experience is empathic.

Of all the fake little houses,
Concealed alone for day and night,
Surrounded by a nothingness.

All these reasons were a cause to fight.

Equality

Winter Wish

In winter times, the chill of ice,
Comes forth to freeze our efforts thrice,
Or more if effort lives alone,
With no one near to call our own.

But here the season justly brings,
Purpose more deep than doing all things;
If effort fails you, time and again,
Rest now, away from the troubles of then.

Be happy in this coming time,
And look to those close by your side-
Closeness that grows, amongst the snow,
All winter wishes surely know.

James Parton

Equality

~ *Love* ~

*"Immature love says: 'I love you because I need you'.
Mature love says: 'I need you because I love you.'"*

– *Erich Fromm*

*No one is worth your tears,
And the one who is won't make you cry.*

– *Unknown*

James Parton

Equality

Love Is…

True love is what you choose it to be,
But I'll tell you what it means to me.

Love is something you feel inside,
Though some people are afraid to confide,
But you should never feel unsure,
If you believe your love is pure.

To me true love is caring and trust,
These two things are a definite must.
Then there's honor, respect with loyalty,
Empathy, rapport, and true maturity.

But first you need to find yourself,
And discover who you are,
As long as you can know yourself,
Your love will take you far.

James Parton

Shimmering State

The flow of your hair,
Caught to the twisting breeze,
Of longing within your soul.

Your hair fell casually,
To your shoulders and sides, to wait;
Your beauty froze, only for that moment,
And held your shimmering state.

I thought these things,
As I saw you simply,
Simple, but complete at the core.

Then through your eyes,
Windows clear as day,
Shone through,
With the light of a thousand stars.

But you laugh and ask me,
"Am I not then too bright to look upon?"

And my answer wavers surely none,
For the degree of my infatuation,
Bends even the rays of the sun.

Equality

Drown in Your Eyes

Of the seas I've seen,
Of the waters abroad,
None are as vast as the one I saw;

Within your eyes,
Into your soul,
Telling the secrets yet to be told.

And within your eyes,
I see the day,
Where somehow I will find my way.

Within your eyes,
I can be content,
Without a word to say.

James Parton

Like the Stars

Our love is like the stars;

Not that it burns out and dies away,
Or falls from space, apart from grace.

Perhaps I get this idea solely because,
The times I am with you,

I feel so far above the world.

Equality

Long Time Crush

5 years so long you thought to know,
Affection in yourself did show,
For edge of all your worldly wants,
Was solely with him to go.

He was confused, much unlike you,
Must have to be such a fool,
To overlook devotion pure;
Let frailty overrule.

I know not what he'll do from now,
Or find his way, no clue of how,
If part from him you must from here,
No longer be devout.

He's lost you while you're always there,
You're far too great to still despair,
So, safe in all your worldly fare,
Bid him due farewell.

James Parton

Can't Find A Way

I just can't find a time to tell you;

Every time the urge to say all these words comes,
The time just isn't right.
I keep waiting for the words to seem easier.

I just can't find the nerve to show you;

Like when we're standing side by side,
And I want only to take your hand in mine, but can't.
I'm too unsure of how you'd react.

I just can't find a way,
To not make my old mistakes…

But can I wait any longer for the right time,
While I put myself through Hell?

While every time I look into your eyes
I want to lose myself for eternity;

While every time I get close to you,
I want to take you in my arms;

Equality

And while every time I think about you,
I want to whisper these words in your ear…

…I want to be with you.

James Parton

Lonely Till Again

Touching with feelings
Long since gone from my soul;

When pain accompanies love and satiation,
For an emptiness.

In missing what means most,
I'm lonely till again you stand beside me.

Equality

Missing You

Memories stand alone,
Close by to a lonely soul,
As sickness rises in my gut.

Where are you?
How are you?
What are you feeling?

Missing you this way,
Release only comes,
With your return.

James Parton

Forgiveness

Above all else,
I only want to be with you.
These words are true to the part of me,
That feels pain when we're apart.

When I look back now, to the past, as it was,
I can't even stand the thought of,
Who I was, what I did,
What I didn't do for you.

And then in my mind, I see so clearly,
That "sorry" just doesn't cut it;
Even if it were good enough for you,
It just isn't good enough for me.

So I have to make things up to you,
Whether you care about the past or not,
And though I'm not the same person as before,
I still remember things that tear apart my soul.

It hurts most because I still miss you,
Because I've had these feelings since the beginning;
Do I feel them even now?
Without a doubt, and stronger still…

Equality

Then the biggest question is why;
Why it took me so long to tell you this,
And why in all the years that I've known you,
I've ruined every opportunity to be with you.

I must have been afraid,
Though it's no excuse,
But a fault of my own,
That I've never dealt with.

I suppose that I worried,
Of what you were thinking, what you were feeling;
There were times I wasn't sure I was even wanted,
And I don't know how right I was.

But I can't be afraid anymore,
That much I can assure you.
Not a single mistake I've made lacked fear,
And I can't change the past.

The most horrible thing about the past,
Is it cannot be changed, sometimes not even repaired.
I only care about what's here and now;
My feelings remain, even if you feel nothing for me,

And even if "sorry" doesn't mean a thing,
I hope the fact that I still love you does.

James Parton

Feelings of You

Tranquil peace pervades my soul,
And my active mind is put to rest;
Looking into your eyes,
I find peace.

Warmth surrounds me,
And kindles my longing;
Holding you in my arms,
I find happiness.

And as we share our warm embrace,
Your lips touch mine;
Nothing else matters,
Except the love that we share.

It is said that no one is perfect,
Until you fall in love with them,
And you, my love,
Are perfect for me.

Equality

Find You There

I'll see you after months to come,
You only need be waiting,
Against the background, setting sun,
All long time pains abating.

I come to search my love alone,
With no one else to bind me,
Forevermore, our perfect own,
Is promised that you find me.

All pasts that be, they be behind,
All obstacles be broken,
Around our lives, in heart and mind,
All words of love are spoken.

And long time be our destiny,
This endless love of you and me.

James Parton

Dreams of Longing

Ice caps melting within the wake,
Of a fire that burned alone,
Content to use my soul as a vessel,
Its home, none less than my own.

So these caps are my bed,
No more icy snow,
Melted emotion,
Still more left to show.

I lie there awake,
With the truths in their rapture,
Seeking release,
From my mind's unknown captor.

It's so within reach,
But a mile within seconds,
The closer to sleep,
It becomes more un-present.

You find me also in my dreams,
For this fire surely lives for,
A constant search, and endless seems,
To never share its candor.

Equality

Such are my calling,
And you're there in forever,
When each dreamed event,
Only truly knows never.

When I wake again,
I wake up alone,
The most vivid dreams,
Are only shown.

These parts that I think
Were caused by my thoughts
To paint their purpose
Never naught.

To get to the bottom,
I suppose I should ask you,
Your dreams as well,
Do they fell and catch you?

I'll show you the path,
To in our own way,
Find a place you can be,
In my arms, come what may.

James Parton

Our History

Before there was you, I was lost in the dark,
Dead to my feelings, dead in my heart.
I had learned the world to be so unjust,
That even my dreams were filled with mistrust,

But the greatest dream, deep within me,
Longed and sought out across the sea.
To my surprise I found you there,
Though it seemed to me you didn't care,

But as we made contact, our love did grow,
Though we were confused, and too blind to know;
Confusion always had its place,
With blissful smiles upon your face.

Then was the day you came to me,
Tears flowing free from a days defeat;
You were troubled as I, and there I was,
To heal your wounds and show you trust.

It was after that day that the feelings exploded,
Among our souls and minds, they floated,
For as your heart would resonate mine,
Our souls connected with careful time.

Equality

But you had your doubts, understandable, really,
While I had experience, understanding fully,
This time was your first, having been alone,
Only my heart, had you been shown.

But fear wouldn't last,
Away your doubts cast,
And unwise as our longing,
Would bind us so strongly.

Now, among the best,
More than we can express,
We'll have each other to hold,
Cherish and grow old,

To love until the end of time…

James Parton

Dreams to Come

Of dreariness,
And sleep's call be,
A deep dream beckons,
Of you and me.

I shouldn't rest,
It's overrated,
But to come to you,
Relief is stated.

So I'll wait till night,
Though I see you today,
And stray toward your light,
To in dreams find my way.

Equality

James Parton

Equality

~ *Pain* ~

"Well, in the end everything works out; so if everything isn't okay, then it's not the end!"

– Leslie Cook

James Parton

Equality

Wondering

If I could take it back,
Things I've said and done,
Perhaps I wouldn't feel so lost.

I'm wondering what you are thinking,
Pondering if I could ever be forgiven.

But will there ever come a time,
When I can forget being worried,
And just be myself?

James Parton

A Game of Those Surrounding

You'll hold your teem ever too close,
while being boisterous so,
Seldom you thought upon the chance,
for any one to know,
Try my best to catch and reveal,
the all you'd never show,
Simple heart, I thought I knew,
would surely never go.

I cannot speak of any things,
that off and end our game,
Until we touch the next degree,
our tuning stays the same,
Yet all around us know our times,
and speak about our fame,
A presence licking, flames of fire,
restlessly untamed.

The growth we need is personal,
apart from all impure,
For all around will cloud the thoughts
and meddle us unsure,
That all you'd ask for is release,
and search about a cure,
Would render you alone in time,
hopeless and demure.

Equality

I never bothered pretending,
to truly know your plea,
The time was sadly rare enough,
you'd ever give to me,
Hence all others, aside from you,
will turn inside to see,
In this world, these things around,
there was no way to be.

James Parton

<u>Filling a Gap</u>

Touching with feelings,
Buried therefore,
Lost in my soul.

Confusion and pain,
Love, satiation,
For an emptiness;

A void once my own.

Equality

Return To Alone

As all of hope would once rise against you,
Free as air, I try to grasp,
Whatever that only I would see,
Of what life entailed.

But what did you expect of me,
If not a mindless perseverance,
To blast away to checkmate,
And see a new day?

Would you rather it be a tale of tell,
Of lesser fight than show,
A death ever silent, impersonal,
To play upon your minds eye?

Given to you I may be at the time,
Such that every day shall pass the same,
Though see as the day, in charge of then,
Returns me to its eternal home,

Where I am once again, as always,
Alone.

James Parton

<u>Games We Play</u>

Games I play,
Defeat I won't taste,
Even if to win,
I decide in haste.

For sometimes made,
A sacrifice must be,
Even to myself forbade,
Though there for all to see.

Equality

Last Resort

He stood upon the ledge,
Contending with suicide.

What was it that haunted his fleeting mind so?
What drove him to such extremes?

No one was around to ask why…
…The exact reason he stood there now.

Nobody cared.

James Parton

Exposed of my Light

Exposed of light,
A mystery how,
Trapped apart,
From solace now.

I've dropped my guard if you so wished,
You seem to have me beat,
And lay myself before you now,
In tribute to defeat.

To get the end, what I so want,
If you permit it so,
If love beget my worldly sin,
I wouldn't let it go.

As now you've trapped me in the light,
From darkness that I'd roam,
So as my sins, my light in life,
Would render me alone.

Equality

Everyone Else's Smile

I caught myself looking at you to find some answer,
For some question that I can't remember;
It left me somehow at the sight of your face.

But if only you'd given me that smile,
That it seems you've given to everyone else;
A beam that even the cruelest words could not turn…

But perhaps you can only give that smile,
When you obviously care; maybe you don't.
I can see how much you enjoy this life,
Having everyone else around;
I can't tell if that did, or ever will include me.

I could just leave, though I know I can't,
And forgive myself for running away from this place;
But I could never seek redemption
If I ran from my feelings.

So I'll stay here and try my best,
Even if it isn't good enough,
And fight all I can for the day I'll find release;
The day I'm the first to receive that smile.

James Parton

Equality

~ *Mind, Body, and Soul* ~

If the doors of perception were cleansed, everything would appear to man as it is, infinite.

– William Blake

James Parton

Equality

All from Fantasy

Dreams explode around me,
When I enter the unconscious realm,
Where sleep is somewhat of a mixed blessing…

I see unmatched fantasy,
That which I wish I could live,
But am tortured that I can't…

It's pent up, these thoughts,
And I need a way to release,
A nagging drive that only grows…

To write, to dance, to sing, to act,
To grow into what plagues my mind,
And seek a final calling…

James Parton

Inspiration to Fight

If a war was declared,
And nobody came,
There'd be no one to fight,
Who wants war anyway?

A man comes to battle with only his life,
Having said goodbye to his kids and his wife.
In hopes of someday once returning,
He considers his past as the world is still turning.

And while he sits there, deep in thought,
He sees the world as quite distraught.
So suddenly it hits him, what he's there to do,
To fight for his life, and his future too.

He says to himself, "I'll never die!"
"As long as deep down, I believe I'm alive!"

Undecided

Your timid brow,
From happens late,
Not like before,
Your hardened state.

A frown or smile,
Which can't decide,
With all the while,
Warred thoughts inside.

So not with me,
Or ever be,
Though sometimes smile,
And there's a chance,

Your choice to never be with me,
A vain filled love, in circumstance.

James Parton

Burning Truth

If all the world be bound in flame,
On to truth and back again,

Back to square one, back to the place,
Where that burning truth shone on my face,

For never the light be dim and died,
A ferocious ego and character alike,

A beacon as if I only shine;
Perhaps this time, it is true.

Equality

Prayer of the Prey

Savage impulses,
Seethe through creatures of pain.

Needn't you worry my child, my pride,
Though fright may seize you in the night.

Strength be to thee through light of mind,
And purest ease of soul.

James Parton

Anticipation

I remember all too well,
The anticipation that tore through to my soul,
And attacked every doubt apparent to its sight.

But through all my uncertainty,
I was confident in my ability:
My ability to not only succeed, but exceed.

The intercom blasted,
Sound flooding the stadium as,
The announcer's proclamation turned my stomach.

"Boy's 1500…1500 meter, boys."
I had stepped cautiously from the stands,
And my feet tread heavily across the asphalt.

The time had come,
I had waited for hours.
And suddenly,

As the runners took their marks,
Got set,
I felt every fear flood from my conscious mind.

Nothing mattered,
I was ready,
'Go!'

Equality

The gun shouted a thunderous reply to my mind,
And signaled the beginning of the race;
A race for my glory and prosperity.

James Parton

Red Pulse

In weariness and lack of power,
No excuses bend to the weak.

If strength be your desire,
Flowing blood as force within the body,

As lonely sorrow, with pulsing exultance,
Rhythm creates your reign.

Equality

High on a Hill

High on a hill,
Seclusion have thee,
Who seek its refuge.

Hermit of silent power,

Strength sought within solitude,
Can be found only upon terrain,
Lonely as such a man

James Parton

Equality

~ *The World* ~

"Until you are content with yourself, you cannot be content with the world."

– *James Parton*

James Parton

Equality

Strength Born of Choice

Humanity can always rely on,
An ability to make choices.

There are infinite possibilities,
In this world we live,
And there will always be,
Those who choose a life of defiance.

Those who exercise the power of choice,
And refuse defeat by anyone or anything:
Such people will forever change the world,
For better or worse.

We learn to welcome such change,
For it cannot be stopped.

James Parton

By the Beach

Roaring lull,
Soothing seas of conscious endearment.

To lay back,
And enjoy such a pleasure,

Oh, to do such a thing;
Life has given you peace.

Equality

Circle of Summer's End

A circle round, around the sky,
Above this cowering place.
A darkness there, all light unfair,
To shine upon my face.

A dream of lovely summer's past,
If permitted something dear,
Yet even amongst these hopes and dreams,
We still give into fear.

James Parton

For After Death

What would I want on my gravestone?

I have to ask,
Would it matter once I'm gone?

When man realizes the magnitude of death,
He begins to worry of being forgotten,
Within the depths of time.

But once death descends upon you,
You needn't worry about such things,
For dead men can do nothing,
About the past, nor for the future;

For they have ceased to exist,
Within this mortal realm,
And have set upon,
A new journey.

People, however, will still try their hardest,
To make a mark on this world,
And be a constant reminder to future generations,

That they made a difference;
Set a higher standard of life.

We can simply live that standard,
Or dare to set a new one…

Equality

Shadowed Hope

Mists of despair,
Looming once before troubled pasts-
To drink them in, wisdom of ages,
Shrouds of darkness overcome.

A shadowy grove,
Not be nigh the light of day-
Crumpled faith in thyself with,
Desolate hope; not lost, but dithering.

Experience becoming thee,
A thought not since apparent-
Death be the scourge to a valiant effort,
Once echoed within the halls of greatness.

Desperate in longing,
Escaping only through satiation-
To roam free on days again,
When light shines hope in your soul.

James Parton

Nations Fallen

Sunlight poised to bring new birth;

Rays of burning desire,
Shine upon the disgrace of nations fallen,

With doom, an amulet of failure.

Carcasses, feasted upon by the winged terrors,
Give monument to all that transpired as of late.

Rule at an end,
Order deceased,
Who will rise to rule again?

~ Epilogue ~

During this journey, love met pain,
Giving the fundamental base of our existence,

The mind, body, and soul found direction,
Learning their dealings between mankind,

And the world came to truly know,
The journeys that explore its complex challenge.

Working from the inside-out,
These themes balance equality in our lives,
And most often leave us grasping for more.

I hope solely that all of these things,
Are present within you,
And that their importance,
Finds a way into your heart.

Equality is…
Our greatest test,
Our truest form,
Our ultimate goal.

About the Author

James Parton lives in Salem, Oregon and attends North Salem High School as a senior, where he studies English literature and composition. He has experimented with poetry and the effects of poetic verse from a young age. "Equality" is his first published work.

CPSIA information can be obtained at www.ICGtesting.com
Printed in the USA
BVOW08s1553120916

461885BV00001B/3/P